Threadbare

Abbie Neale

smith|doorstop

Published 2020 by Smith|Doorstop Books
The Poetry Business
Campo House,
54 Campo Lane,
Sheffield S1 2EG
www.poetrybusiness.co.uk

ISBN 978-1-912196-27-2
Designed & Typeset by Utter
Printed by Biddles

Acknowledgements

I'd like to thank everyone at The Poetry Business – Ann and Peter Sansom, Ellen McLeod, Suzannah Evans, Eleanor Holmshaw, Katie McLean and Jess Timperley – for helping me bring my first publication into existence! A million thank yous to Mary Jean Chan for choosing me as one of the winners. Thank you to Jack McGowan, David Morley and Jonathan Skinner, who all believed in this collection, and to Tundun Obidipe, for taking the photo on the cover. And finally: thanks to my wonderfully supportive parents and sisters, and lovely Jozsi.

Smith|Doorstop books are a member of Inpress:
www.inpressbooks.co.uk. Distributed by NBN International, 1 Deltic Avenue, Rooksley, Milton Keynes, MK13 8LD.

The Poetry Business gratefully acknowledges the support of
Arts Council England.

Contents

Part One

7   The feeding

8   Can you draw him for us

10   We saw all of it

12   What the women wore

14   Red

15   The neighbours know

16   Buttermilk

17   The bed in Bea's room

18   'I thought you were into it'

19   Stuart's highway

20   In a parked car he drives

21   When I walked out

Part Two

25   Miracles are brought

26   Between two clouds

28   In my thinking of you

30   The first time since the last time

31   A spectacle in the green hills

32   Long distance

33   Being told that you are loved

34   Reclaiming the word

35   For my sister

36   Painting my mother

*Dedicated to Mum, who still sews the holes
in my clothes (and my heart).*

PART ONE

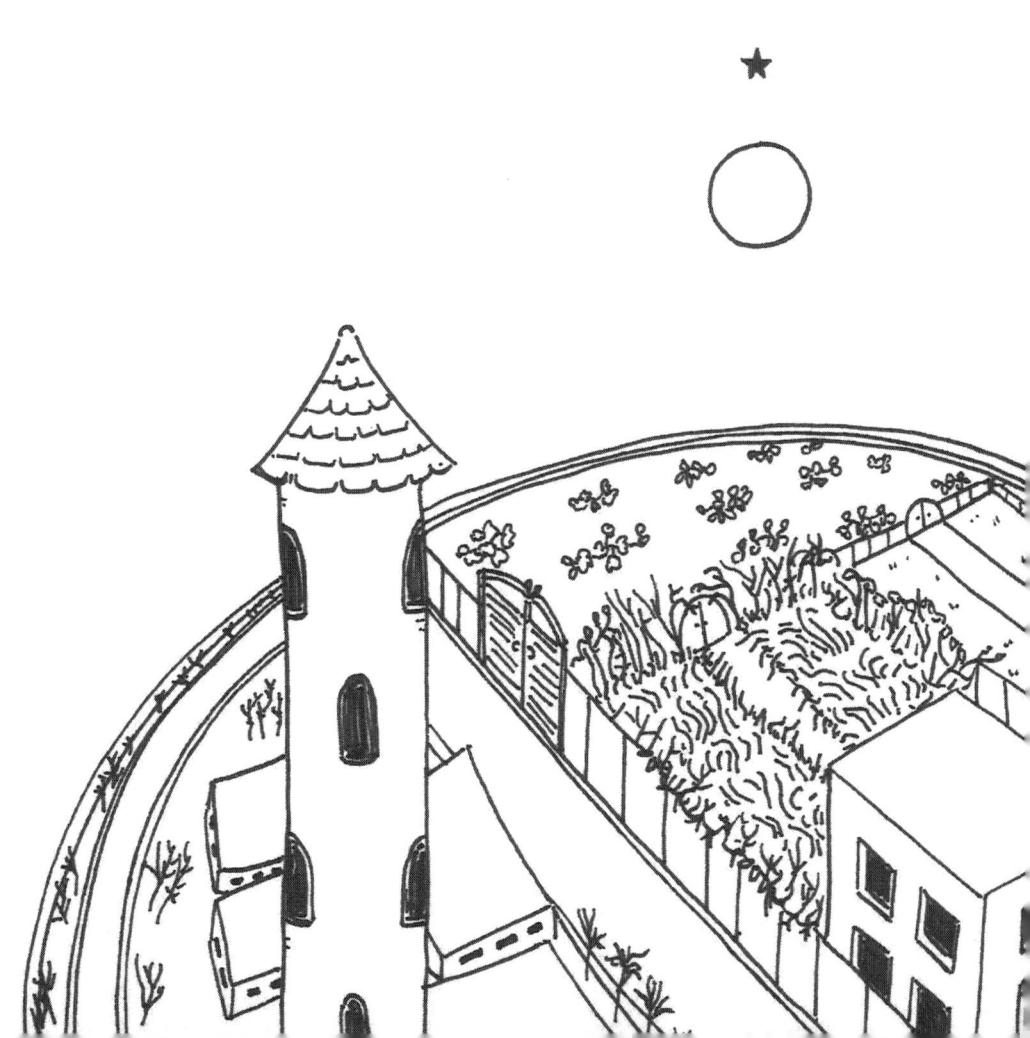

The feeding

Our mother never eats.
Perhaps she is fed in secret.

She says that a goldfinch keeps her alive
but Bea thinks it's the men.

I like the one who comes downstairs.
He gives me high fives and high tens.

They always forget to wake her up
and they blacken her cotton wool.

She must eat what the men give her.
Her throat is bruised from all the eating

and her feet drag when she's full.
Bea doesn't like the new one.

He hums like he has pipes in him
and it makes her fingertips tingle.

We sit some evenings in the same room
and he asks us if we mind.

We don't reply in case it's a trigger
for him to get hateful or rude

but I'm scared if we leave it
he might get bigger,

like mould on an old bit of food.

Can you draw him for us

Bea rolls the nose of a ballpoint
across paper, mapping her walk
home from school to the police.

She details the ducks, daisies
and buttercups. When she draws
the traffic lights she pauses,

talks about ducks again because
ducks aren't the scary part.
There's no green for the wings

so she outlines the lamp post instead
where she saw the man waiting.
It cranes over him like a surrealist

showerhead. She pretends to probe
the beige plush carpet to show
how she picked the flowers

like a sandpiper pecking for prey.
The man didn't go.
Bea says she walked towards him

because that was the way home.
She didn't want his smile
or his sweets so he tripped her

and that's when she ran.
Our mother's mouth falls open.
The feeble noise that escapes

8

makes Bea give the pen back
and a quiet panic settle
in her throat, like feathers.

We saw all of it

Kids bullying kids for being simple, or simply doing sums,
the waiting gates for bully-dads and bully-mums,

Kids rating kids on their 'things' and their looks,
in the library making out (and taking out anything but books).

Kids telling kids to *do it* or *don't do it*
and those pretending not to know, even when they knew it.

This is what we saw as we peeped from our tower
at kids spilling like mustard seeds, brown and yellow,

out the school gates and into the orchard below.
I pictured the oranges, how the children never touched them,

never even tried, and how it felt to be shaken only by
the hands of the wind and only hit by the light, just right,

a shine on their curve, as if each one held a moon inside.
A knot formed in my throat as I watched on, out of earshot,

wondering what they'd say, day and night;
the kids to other kids, the trees to their baubles

and over time the garden grew and the knot there thickened
as we waited for a child to prod, punch or pick them.

But they listened to their fathers and mothers, and stayed away.
I prayed one day they'd do the same for each other,

ask before they hit, rough-and-tumbled, touched, shook
and leave what isn't theirs like the fruit,

like the undiscovered dust-covered library books.

What the women wore

On a coat hanger, a bathrobe
rests against his bedroom door.
He enjoys them nylon or silk,
shawl or kimono, open-fronted
and opposite his bed, so he can
imagine the women inside them.

This one is blue, tight-fitting
and lighter than the others.
When our mother first stayed
with him, it was a pink dressing
gown, long and loose, lined
with fleece for the winter nights,

that she donned like it was hers.
For their bitter cold breakfasts
the robe was always there, until
she learnt the name of the wearer,
the woman who came before
and it didn't feel right anymore

so she bought the pastel blue.
No cotton velour, no cashmere
wrap, but a housecoat worn
in the day too, quilted and cool
for any occasion, like the morning
he woke and told her it was over.

'It's blue,' said Mum, rifling
through the box that he left outside.
We found no clothes. Her brow
furrowed, then a hollow laugh rose
from deep within. 'It's with him.'
What lady paraded our mother

around, sipping from the same mug,
slipping on the same knitted socks
he offered her? Mum recalled how
she'd put on the pink, a little bit smug,
secretly pleased that she was the one
with her hands inside of its pockets.

Red

Sheltering from the rain outside, where
the thunder moves fast but the sun falls in

slow motion. From our tower we see
a man under a storefront, waiting, pacing

and smoking as if he's embarrassed to be
smoking. There's a lake in the distance

like tin foil hiding an entire existence
and carrying tiny boats. Close is a boy on

a bike, riding to a girl in a shiny red coat.
It's an oil painting on a canvas, thinned by

rainwater and his wheels spin colours
and the picture changes. Next, the girl is

given something, maybe a bracelet, so she
embraces the boy, kisses him between

the ears and it appears to be
forgiveness and the image is comforting.

Inside, in the rosy light of a child's curiosity,
on her tiptoes, a mild cough and runny nose,

my sister finds a book of bedtime stories.
She asks if it'll stop raining, and then if Little

Red should give the wolf a second chance
because he looks so daft in Grandma's clothes

and the poor thing must have been starving.

The neighbours know

I read somewhere that the star was called
Venus. It hovered alone above the moon
which was our very own faraway lighthouse.
The tower overlooked the city

and the trees which flowered, shading
the streets, and we prayed for the woman
in the house next door and the garden
that used to be pretty.

We caught a man in the window once and
thought he might have lived there
and when they came outside the night
flourished, blooming like the nearby orchard,

but their garden lacked love, wiry and tired,
there were cracks in their plant pots
where the weeds pushed through, alive and
wild and tortured.

We weren't expecting what happened next,
what demanded to be seen; it flashed
in our eyes and clung to our lashes and
the woman didn't scream or fight.

It penetrated everything, this silent sight
wasn't private, not in a garden where
the moon shone like satin, like the delicate
frills that hung there to dry overnight.

Buttermilk

Pinned to the wall is a person, drawn by a child.
She has a woman's body with soft crayon edges.

In the picture, the sun is an oval, as if someone
has thrown a Mirabelle plum into the air

and it is about to hit her. Whoever's room this is
must be out of the house, and does not know

I am here. He told me we'd be making pancakes
and I believed him. He talked of his parents,

I thought I would meet them. But the bedrooms
are empty and he shows me them one by one.

There isn't time to take off my glasses. I can see
the textured ceiling, like painted popcorn kernels,

and the particles of dust – tiny fibres, carpet lint,
our hair and skin floating like petals and burnt

meteorites. And I can see the end of my nose.
I wonder what would happen if I breathed

in all of it: soil and plant pollen, lead, arsenic.
I imagine it churning in my brain and stomach.

It's on the train home that I see the blood. I smile
because that means it worked. Like packaged eggs,

cream-coloured, deep brown, pink and speckled,
we've learnt that we are better broken. It will hurt

for a few days he said, and in the toilet I clean
beneath my legs, delighted to have been chosen.

The bed in Bea's room

Where he waited for her fever to pass,
where he laughed at her threadbare sheets,
where he showed her City and Colour,
where they entwined legs and touched feet.

Where she let him unzip himself, his hand
on her head, barbed nails pressing down.
She would not upset him or flounder about,
startled and hooked from one eyebrow.

She wasn't sure what they had both let happen
in the threadbare bed in her room,
where she felt for her blanket like a seat belt
as she worked up the courage to ask him.

It's not my fault, he breathed, *you were part
of it too* and she knew what that implied.
She'd watch him smile, and she wore it herself
for a while, like a shirt with the tag still inside.

'I thought you were into it'

He says it holding a vodka lime,
looking into the glass,
probably thinking about *passion*.
I remember a navel bite mark.
Ocean's Eleven, the remake.
A machete collection, his dad's.
In case we made a baby,
he doesn't tell me his last name.
It's like we both forget I'm there.
It will be four years until I learn
that something can be consensual
and wrong at the same time.
He looks up from the vodka lime.
There's space between us now
like two sides of a bascule bridge,
a yawn spawned from a kiss,
a learned loneliness.
Enough space to contemplate
the meaning of *into it*, of him
laughing and me joining in,
of a straw that moves in slow
circles, stirring the floaters
in my eyes, like cat hairs.

Stuart's highway

The roadside is vast, orange,
eating into the highway and burning
the belly of their parked car.

She follows him to the train tracks
for the better view he promised
to see the rocks cling to the horizon

like giant fingertips, to see the road
shimmer like glass-case opals,
but mostly to stop him drinking.

* * *

He throws condoms into the fire
and she says *no* and *stop it*
when he pretends to throw her on it.

Calm down. With her so close
he goes for the can of Silly String
despite her screaming.

After the explosion he lets
the campfire cool, gold, blue,
spilling upwards into the night.

In a parked car he drives

into her repeatedly
and the promise of love
letters disappears
behind two powdery
black dragon-fruit eyes.

He finishes over her
leg, and for some reason
she says sorry, then asks
him for permission
to open a window.

When I walked out

I didn't make it very far. On the driveway, there was space
to come apart because no one was home when it happened.

The only cars were the ones that passed, the drive was as bare
as the cast-iron sky and both were beginning to blacken.

Collapsing means falling. Down, over, inwards. It also means
an abrupt loss of perceived value. I thought of all the sprawled

people who were made to feel small, like my mother when he left,
how it could take months to fold but seconds to fall.

I found her in the shower, unconscious. She had left her body
in her attempts to find him. That's where I was going, I knew it.

When I fell, the trees and houses were geometric shapes
and I didn't hit the ground, I tore through it.

PART TWO

Miracles are brought

The old lady ambles up the path, where a sapling grows
in the black earth, where it hurts, where it happened.

This house dressed in green, between the orchard
and the school, brings guests of all kind – nesting

blackbirds, and her. Like the seeds of a dandelion
her hair comes out in wisps, blessing the ground

that was once withered. Those who pass it
see the baskets she leaves, hanging from the trees,

perky blossoms dangling, demanding to be seen.
Through the backdoor, the pockets of sunlight

warm the hardwood floor and expose the dust
drifting in like flakes of snow. The sweeping

drifts of snowdrops shake in the wind as she waits
for her daughter, swaying in the morning serenade.

Between two clouds

We talked in our big voices
about the black sky
between interstellar clouds,
about the shadow space
between the stars and yet
Bea stayed in the car while
I watched the moon, full
and orange, and rising

over the dunes, the surface
of a split-open runway –
the salt lake, the tent poles
over cities, mountains,
the backs of trees
overpowering waterfalls,
all she said was:
I wish it never happened.

We never talked about how
the cracks in our teacups
and coffee dregs are now
simply leftovers,
never talked about her ex,
or sex without pain
or how the rain is warmer
when she's with me

or how one might split the custody
of a vegetable garden
spinach, sunflower, bucket bean,
about how we wept
in separate rooms,
hoping to be heard by the other.
In this new place the windows
are bigger, the curtains are open.

In my thinking of you

You leap in a meadow
　　or some sprung boggy marsh
glowing like buttered honey toast
sliced lemon, spicy tea
　　and the sun –
you shield your eyes with fingers and thumb
a hover fly landing, as I wish to land
on your physical outstretched hand.

I tell my sister about the heron
　　the memory swelling
how it was gone by the time we reached
　　the river.
She jokes about us in our canvas shoes
filling with pond puddles and mudhole soup
and the thought of *the frogs!*
　　makes her shiver.

I burrow into bed
　　her kneeling beside it
reeling from this: my *happy day.*
That's what she calls it
as she strokes the blush from my cheeks
wondering
　　out loud
when she'll get to meet you.

But it's hard to hear her –
I'm back in the grass
   the sun has set.
We laugh as we tread
trying to dodge the snails in the dark
wading the barracks of their tiny army
   alarmed
squirming at each murderous crack of a shell.

The first time since the last time

My limbs are long and thin, like the bones in a bat's wing,
a polyester membrane spread between them on the bed.

I think about covering them. You would not like to see me
in the daytime, my naturally skittish, spindly spider body.

But when you emerge from your tissue cocoon, your eyes
flicker, perceiving an ultraviolet, polarised light that I can't.

At first, I wince at the thought of flowers. *Beautiful, delicate.*
Plucked. Washed. Ready to devour. He saw me as something

to set alight, outside and in, so I cut myself above the skin,
learnt to strip it all for him. Yet here you are,

loving the parts that he never could, touching me gently,
almost not touching, like the sensory hairs on a butterfly.

A spectacle in the green hills

We're a pack when we run, a flurry of rain macs
converging on the Himalayan tents.
We are whipping through summer's waters
like wind-blown bin bags with twinkling eyes,
stripping ourselves, unveiling and flailing
in a celebration of ridiculous limbs,
offering them to the Babylon Circus,
summiting each sonority peak
with a howl to the electric lights.
We are the spots on the trout's skin, weaving in
and out of the people, dotted and shining.
Silk ribbons fly from festival trees,
slender bodies with psychedelic jazz hands
and you are sporting a coat to your knees,
sun visor and smile, beer cans and cardboard chips.
It's for all of this that I fall towards you,
my fawn of a heart straining, eyes open,
into your arms where it bleats, hungry at last.

Long distance

A waving arm, an open palm, a goodbye.
At the station, I choose to remember this:
as the guard beckons and seconds slip by,
there's a nose bump and a bristly kiss.

At the station, I choose to remember this:
the way we laugh but our hearts aren't in it,
the nose bump and bristly kiss,
the flirt with time, the hurtling minutes.

So we're laughing but our hearts aren't in it,
the words we don't say weigh on us like rain,
we're flirting with time, our hurtling minutes,
you bow your flat cap as I board the train.

The words we don't say weigh on us like rain,
the guard beckons and the seconds slip by,
you bow your flat cap as I board the train.
A waving arm, an open palm: another goodbye.

Being told that you are loved

It doesn't hit me at first. The telling of it,
we've learnt, is not all that rare – but the
deep-seated knowing, the feeling it's there
is like the navel embossing from your belt
buckle, my lying on you, like the bathing
chase of the sun across the garden, the bass
guitar drum-beating backbone of the soul
song, carefree Al Green. It's the closeness
of roasted coffee bean handfuls, it's danger
and relief, it's the hairless tail escaping the
bird beak – and then it hits me, and it keeps
hitting me, big as raindrops to a field mouse.

Reclaiming the word

The forest where we fucked looks even better in the daytime,
the bluebells bend over, begging sunlight to lick their backs.
I can now say *fuck* without feeling uneasy. It used to remind
me of terrible dreams: phallic office telephones and pay gaps,

a commitment I made whilst I was asleep, socks eating feet,
secretly nibbling at pages of weekly weight-loss magazines,
sexual anxiety, a gaping orifice where the clock should be,
pussy-grabs, mouthfuls of crabapples and curdled screams.

Today I cling to the word like ivy, sing it like the blackbird
sings from the treetops down to the waterfowls in the reeds.
I suck the tips of the spreading purple perennial and serve
myself up, like the rain in the curved spoon-shaped leaves.

For my sister

The Old Lady faces the lake, cross-legged, her back to us.
'I'm the part of you that's weary. The part that no one trusts.'

Visitors of the graveyard, we halt at the sound of her voice.
She thinks we're brave for coming, but we didn't have a choice.

She says, without turning, 'You're the women who survived.'
Her hair is caught, not by the wind, but by the fireflies.

They puppeteer and pull at it, like stars to the stark grey moon.
Before we forward march, she stands: 'I think I'll be leaving soon.

'Thank the ones who believe your words and love you back to life.
Listen to the blackbirds. Build a house for the blackbird's wife.'

Our tears flow into the lake, growing underwater forests.
'Tomorrow, it'll be sunny,' she says. 'And that, I can promise.'

Painting my mother

It is saddest when it stops me painting.
I'm well acquainted with a square paintbrush head
and the faint murmur of pigeons in the morning
but this week the wind, like a warning, blew
down my chimney and it came with the cold
and my fingers didn't know how to hold it anymore.
Until I spoke to her. I confessed it in the car of all places
because that way she couldn't look at me.
She knew this type of pain, she had felt it too
and when she parked in the driveway we stayed there
for hours, talking it through.
That night I thought how lucky I was to be loved by her
and slept like a baby curled in the womb.
I woke, and there were plant leaves on the table, poppies
and safflowers and a circle of linseed and walnuts
in the living room. The oil was boiled with pine resin
in unlined steel cans, the canvas was ready
and for the first time in a while my hands were steady.
I worked without a chair, and the wind was still there, but
now I liked how it made the paint bend in the air.
Her cheeks and her chin I made red,
and the dripping blue that came from her head
moved to her shoulders and undulating chest,
creating the shape of an S, and dipped into the plains
of her belly. Then into the sweeping brushstrokes
of her face I added two eyes, parchment-white,
like the blossoms that floated in through the fireplace
and three coats of varnish to let the artwork harden.
I was her daughter, I was a woman
in a Waterhouse garden.